SERMON OUTLINES
ON
The Book
of John

BEACON SERMON OUTLINE SERIES

SERMON OUTLINES
ON
The Book of John

GENE WILLIAMS

Beacon Hill Press of Kansas City
Kansas City, Missouri

Copyright 2002
by Beacon Hill Press of Kansas City

ISBN 083-411-9889

Printed in the
United States of America

Cover Design: Paul Franitza

Library of Congress Cataloging-in-Publication Data

Williams, Gene, 1932
  Sermon outlines on the book of John / Gene Williams.
    p. cm. — (Beacon sermon outline series)
  ISBN 0-8341-1988-9 (pbk.)
  1. Bible. N.T. John—Sermons—Outlines, syllabi, etc. I. Title. II. Series.
  BS2615.54.W55 2002
  251'.02—dc21

2002009223

10   9   8   7   6   5   4   3   2   1

Contents

Introduction

Food from John's Gospel

If a person could only have one book from God's Word, the Gospel of John would be a great choice. While the beauty of the Christmas story is not recorded there, the simple story of the life, ministry, and message of Jesus is inscribed throughout the entire book.

More than any other book in the Bible, John draws attention to the love of God. One does not get lost in a lot of theological jargon but is rather drawn over and over to Jesus and His shepherd love. These sermon outlines are planned with God's guidance to bring a congregation to this focus. In so doing, they cannot help but confront the listener with the love of God as revealed in Jesus. And that kind of love is hard to resist.

I believe that those who already know Him will be greatly encouraged by revisiting God's love for them. I also believe that those who do not know Him will want to meet Him. It is very difficult to walk away from God's love once it has truly been demonstrated.

You will notice that most of these messages grow out of a lengthy passage of scripture. In some cases the entire chapter is considered. This is by deliberate design. While the messages are not exegetical in nature, I believe we have nothing to say that is as important as the Word of God, hence the long passages. If the messages were placed in a category, they would be classified as "needs centered."

While any sermon can be isolated from the others, there is an advantage in keeping them in series. The congregation will become more involved in reading the Word in anticipation of the message for the coming week.

Take these seeds, water them with prayer, and see what God causes to grow in your fertile heart and mind.

The One Who Came

John 1:1-29

Introduction

  A. There is a lot of misunderstanding about Jesus and who He is in our world today.

  1. Many of the cults thrive on half-truths by paying only lip service to Jesus.

  2. There are those who call themselves Christians but do not respond to Jesus as the divine Son of God.

  3. There are those who believe but who are not excited about Jesus.

  4. There are the people who have a genuine love for Him. Everything in their lives revolves around Jesus.

  B. We are going to take a look at God's Word with the goal of getting to know Jesus better. Who was this Man who came and made such an impact on the world for all time? Read John 1:1-29.

  C. There are two important language notes to be considered. The verb "was" is used three times to describe continuous action without regard to beginning or ending. "Word" speaks of the essential nature of God—His self-disclosure.

I. Jesus Is Divine (vv. 1 and 14)

  A. The Gospels introduce Jesus in different ways: Matthew—Joseph's Son, a descendent of Abraham and David (see 1:1-16); Luke—Mary's Son conceived by the Holy Ghost (see 1:26-38); Mark—Jesus, "the Son of God" (1:1); John—Jesus is divine (17:5).

  B. Since Jesus is God, we will want to pay serious attention to Him.

II. He Is Light (John 1:5, 8, 9)

  A. Jesus is the Light of the World.

B. What is the role of light? To drive back the darkness; remove uncertainty; show us a way of safe travel.

C. Jesus is the Light that leads us into the Father's presence.

1. He is saying, "This is the way to the Father."

2. You cannot make it so dark but what light can drive it back.

III. Jesus Is Fullness (v. 16)

A. One of the characteristics of the Gospel is the completeness that is found in Jesus.

1. What Jesus is involved in is more than adequate.

2. Illustrate with the miracle of turning water to wine, multiplication of fish, etc.

B. Our lives are constantly kept fresh because of Him.

IV. Jesus Is Worthy of Our Worship (v. 27)

A. John is clearly exalting Jesus (see vv. 15, 26-27).

1. Look at verse 15. He uses the testimony of John the Baptist to do this.

2. Again in verses 26-27, he quotes John the Baptist lifting up Jesus.

B. Jesus is worthy to be the Lord of our lives.

1. Some people come to Him as though they are doing Him a favor.

2. What is your attitude toward Him?

V. Jesus Is God's Forgiving Sacrifice (v. 29)

A. The word "lamb" had special meaning to the Jews. Because a lamb gave its life, they could leave the temple forgiven.

B. Jesus is the ultimate sacrifice for our sins.

1. There is a solution to the sin problem in our lives—Jesus, God's Lamb.

2. There is freedom for us because of the price He paid.

Conclusion

The One who came made a dramatic difference in the lives of John's readers. John the Baptist directed his hearers to Jesus and many followed Him. What will you do with Jesus?

The Best Is Yet to Come

John 2:1-11

Introduction

    A. This is the beginning of the public ministry of Jesus.

    B. This passage begins a series of miracles that comprises about one-third of John's Gospel.

        1. The record starts with the turning of water into wine and climaxes in the raising of Lazarus from the dead.

        2. There is a constantly recurring theme of contrasts showing that those who follow the way of Jesus have the best available experiences in front of them.

    C. Some people have a problem with the fact that Jesus turned water to wine. It cannot be interpreted to give support to the insane consumption of alcohol. The point of the miracle is that for those who are obedient to His guidance, the best is yet to come. Read John 2:1-11. Note four lessons in this miracle.

I. Jesus Cares for the Total Life of All Humankind (vv. 1-2)

    A. In that day weddings were the main social events of the communities. Friends and family would gather. Sometimes festivities would last for days.

    B. There are three things to remember: (1) Jesus cares about the total life of all people; (2) Jesus wants all of us to enjoy the normal pleasures of life; (3) miserable Christians are poor advertisements.

II. We Must Learn to Tell Jesus About Every Need (v. 3)

    A. We need to learn to talk with Jesus about every aspect of our lives. Mary felt free to state her concern and leave it with Him.

    B. Jesus is concerned about everything in your life.

III. The Key to Jesus' Best Is Found in Obedience (vv. 5-8)

A. Jesus' instructions were simple.
1. Fill the water pots. These were large clay jars of 17-18 gallons each.
2. They filled them to the limit of what they could hold.
3. Their obedience resulted in maximum benefits.

B. Jesus' exerts His power over nature.
1. The manner that Jesus uses to accomplish his miracles is immaterial. That's what makes them miracles.
2. The very nature of a miracle is the setting aside of normal processes.

C. The route to Jesus' best is simple—obedience.
1. We do not need to understand. Jesus did not explain any miracle to anyone.
2. Those who experience the beautiful things He has planned for them simply obey His instructions.

IV. Those Who Obey Jesus Have the Best Part of Their Lives in Front of Them (v. 10)

A. This is one of the dramatic differences between the two lifestyles set out before all of us. Sin of necessity sets forth its best in the beginning. Sin costs little at the beginning but tightens the noose as time passes.

B. Paul said, "No eye has seen, no ear has heard, no mind has conceived what God has prepared for those who love Him" (1 Cor. 2:9). Isaiah said, "If you are willing and obedient, you will eat the best from the land" (1:19). No human power can imagine the wonderful things God has prepared for His people.

Conclusion

Here is one final lesson: Jesus makes no room for, has no patience with, hypocrisy (John 2:13-16). But those who are obedient and honest have a great future with Him.

The Basics of Being a Christian

John 3:1-17

Introduction

A. We are looking at one of the best-known passages of scripture in the Bible. It contains one of the first verses we ever learned. Verses 1-10 focus on being born again; verses 14-17, on God's love for the world.

B. We want to keep everything in the picture. There are three basic truths that are very important for us to remember if we are ever to become all that God wants us to be. Read John 3:1-17.

I. Basic Truth No. 1: Being Religious Is Not Enough to Get Us to Heaven

A. Look at Nicodemus. He was a member of the supreme religious order of the day. "Pharisee" implies a "separated one." If he were alive today, he would have a perfect church attendance record. As a well-educated believer, he needed something else (vv. 2-3).

B. What does it mean to be born again? It is more than turning over a new leaf or making a resolution to improve one's life. It is a radical, life-changing experience. In that experience, our old sinful, imprisoned life is changed (see 2 Cor. 5:17).

II. Basic Truth No. 2: Becoming a Christian Is Simple

A. We have an aversion for simple things.

B. Jesus illustrated the simplicity of being delivered with a story from the Old Testament (see John 3:14-15 and Num. 21).

1. The children of Israel were in the desert between Egypt and Canaan (see Num. 21).

2. Deliverance was provided for everyone.

3. Those who simply looked in faith lived. Those who did not died.

4. Jesus is saying to Nicodemus, "Deliverance is available and simple to realize."

C. Deliverance from the curse of sin comes by looking in faith to Jesus: (1) we acknowledge our need for deliverance; (2) we look in faith to Jesus for salvation; (3) eternal life is irrefutably tied to a person's dependence upon Jesus.

III. Basic Truth No. 3: God Paid a Price So That We Might Have Eternal Life

A. God sent Jesus to pay the price for our forgiveness from sin.

1. The sacrifice for sin was made when the high priest went into the holy of holies with the blood of a perfect lamb (note Heb. 9:11-14; 10:16-22).

2. Jesus is the perfect Lamb slain for our sins.

3. The only way to be a Christian is to let Jesus be our Savior.

B. Do not stop at John 3:16. Note verse 17. Jesus came and was lifted up to enable us to enjoy the best life available to humankind.

Conclusion

A. Nicodemus was a good man, but there was an emptiness in his life.

1. How can that emptiness be filled?

2. Come to Jesus. Start a new life in the power of His love.

B. There are good people listening who have an empty spot.

1. Nothing can satisfy that void like Jesus.

2. In simple faith, come to Him today.

WELCOME TO THE WELL

John 4:1-30

Introduction

A. This passage of scripture speaks to a major portion of the world's population. They are frustrated by life and are mocked by things that are supposed to make life meaningful. They go from one experience to the next with little hope of finding fulfillment. The message of this passage speaks plainly to that need. Read John 4:1-30.

B. Here are some interesting side notes:

1. It is very obvious that Jesus and John the Baptist were not in competition with each other. Since John was ministering in Judea, Jesus went to the Galilee area. They were not rivals. John said, "He must increase, but I must decrease" (3:30, KJV).

2. It states in 4:4, "Now he had to go through Samaria." Most Jews avoided this area. The Samaritans were the product of intermarriage, of Jews compromising with the hated Babylonians during the captivity.

3. Although Jesus was divine, He was also human and became physically weary (v. 6).

I. Jesus Cares for Everyone (vv. 7-9, 27)

A. In John 3 we learn that He cares for highly educated, wealthy, well-respected people.

B. In John 4 we read that He demonstrated His caring for those at the other end of the social spectrum. In verse 9 we read that the woman was surprised Jesus would even speak to her. Women of that day had no real status in the society. Christianity has done more for women than any other religion or ideology. The scripture evidence points to a woman of loose morals. Jesus made it a habit to reach out to sinners in all walks of life.

C. Jesus still cares for everyone.

II. Jesus Knows Everything That Has Ever Happened in Your Life (vv. 16-18, 28-29)

A. He knew everything that had happened in this woman's life. He knew she had been married five times. He knew she was living in immorality at the time of their encounter. Jesus knew all of that. Yet He had compassion on her.

B. Jesus knows everything in your life.

III. Jesus Offers Permanent Satisfaction (vv. 13-14)

A. Her lifestyle did not satisfy.

B. The gift of Jesus is always new and never grows old. In verses 13 and 14 the language for the water is the same word we would use for an artesian well that constantly springs up with freshness. The flow cannot be stopped. You can only divert it. But it will roll on.

C. The woman had an external religion that allowed her to continue in her sins but did not meet the deepest needs of her soul.

IV. It Is Simple to Enjoy a Satisfying Life (vv. 28-30, 39-42)

A. First, we must listen to what is being said. The woman finally listened to Jesus. The people listened to her testimony.

B. Second, we must believe what we hear. She did (v. 29), and her life was changed. While the people knew how she was living, she finally acknowledged it and was changed. The people listened to what she said, and they were changed as well (vv. 40-42). Their village was transformed because of the new well of everlasting life that had sprung up and would never go dry.

Conclusion

The well of continuous satisfaction is available today. You are invited to know the beauty of a contented soul. Follow the example of this nameless woman who left a life of frustration and defeat to experience satisfaction and victory.

Help for Hurting People

John 5:1-16

Introduction

A. There may have never been a time in the history of humankind when so many people hurt so much. There have always been hurting people. How can we say that they are hurting more today? The things that are supposed to satisfy have in reality become chains around the necks of people. Medical discoveries have only lengthened the misery. Conveniences do not solve those needs.

B. The reason for this is that nothing can meet the deepest needs of humankind except Jesus.

C. Read John 5:1-16. Note: (1) The pool is just inside the gate that leads to Bethany that was used by many shepherds. (2) A walk from Jerusalem to Bethany takes a person over the Mount of Olives and into the Sheep Gate. (3) Shepherds stopped there to water their sheep on the way to the market. (4) For some reason Jesus' attention was drawn to a man lying by the pool. Consider these three lessons in this encounter.

I. There Are No Hopeless Cases with Jesus (vv. 5-7)

A. If there ever was a hopeless case, this one qualified. The man had been sick for 38 years and had been there many times. The water had been troubled frequently, but he was never quite able to get into the water in time. Whatever this man's problem, Jesus changed all of it that day. This was not the only time Jesus healed an impossible case (see Luke 8:43).

B. There are no hopeless cases with Jesus today. Sometimes Jesus solves the problem. Other times He makes us strong enough to live with the situation (see 2 Cor. 12:9-10).

II. The Key to Getting Help Is to Genuinely Want It (John 5:6)

A. Jesus determined the man sincerely wanted out of his misery. Some people would rather complain than be healed. Jesus wanted to be sure the man had not gotten accustomed to his condition to the point of enjoying it. Jesus cuts through all the excuses and defenses to the real issue. He asks, "Do you want to get well?"

B. This is a question we must answer when grappling with our hurts and problems. Do I really want a solution to my problems? Those who genuinely want out make no demands for their deliverance. They leave that to God. The desire for help can apply to marriage problems, health issues, overcoming grief, and all other areas.

III. Help Comes to Those Who Believe Jesus (vv. 8-9)

A. When was this man healed? Healing came when he took Jesus at His word. Jesus told him what to do, and he did it. Note: He was *immediately* made well (v. 9). Jesus did not touch him or help him get up. Jesus does not do for us what we can do for ourselves.

B. The procedure has not changed. There is help for us when we take Jesus at His word. Too often we want to see the evidence of help before we believe.

Conclusion

A. There are three lessons from this story for us to remember.

1. There is help for every situation in our lives.

2. We must truly believe that Jesus can help us.

3. We must respond with immediate obedience.

B. Jesus helps hurting people.

1. He will either remove the load or make you stronger.

2. Either way He chooses to respond with the help that is needed to make our lives better.

More than Adequate

John 6:1-13

Introduction

A. One of the major obstacles that prevents many Christians from experiencing the joy of knowing that God has used them is the "I could never do that" syndrome. They let Satan intimidate them and keep them from stretching themselves for God. The question is not one of adequacy or ability but one of availability to God. When people are available to God, the responsibility for success shifts from them to Him. Illustration: Look at what happened with Moses in Exod. 3 and 4.

B. Today's scripture illustrates that our call is to be available to our God who makes us more than adequate. Read John 6:1-13.

C. There is a powerful truth to be remembered. You can keep what you have, use it on yourself, and end up with nothing. Or you can give yourself and what you have to God and keep that forever. Consider these observations.

I. God Uses Unlikely Sources

A. In order to appreciate the miracle, we need to understand the situation.

1. Following the miracle in John 5, Jesus went to the area around the Sea of Galilee to rest.

2. A crowd was constantly following Him (see 6:2-3).

3. The disciples wanted to send them away, but Jesus cared too much to let that happen. They had a major problem (see v. 7).

B. Note the source for the solution to the problem (v. 8).

1. The answer came from the least likely source (v. 9).

2. The little boy was the last one who would have been considered to have the solution.

3. He is nameless so that any one of us can step into that role of being used by God.

II. Nothing Is Inadequate in Jesus' Hands

A. Andrew pointed out the inadequacy of the little boy's lunch (v. 9).

1. A look at the boy's lunch would have convinced anyone that it was barely enough for one person.
2. Five thousand men, not counting women and children, with *this* lunch? The key was that the lad gave all he had to Jesus.

B. God has placed in all of nature the ability to do more than the mind can comprehend.

1. One grain of wheat can eventually lead to the planting of an entire field.
2. That which is consumed on self is through being productive.
3. Any obedient person can do anything God wants him or her to do.

III. Whatever God Uses Is More than Enough (vv. 12-13)

A. God always exceeds just meeting the need.

1. In Mark 8 when Jesus fed the 4,000, there were seven "basketfuls" left over (v. 8).
2. In Luke 5, both boats were filled to overflowing (see v. 7).

B. How does a person know the plenitude of God?

1. Obedience is the key.
2. Everyone who experienced the overflow did so because he or she had obeyed the guidance of Jesus.

Conclusion

God is looking for some lunches to multiply. Can He have yours? If you give Him what you have, you will have more than you need in the days to come. There is great joy in knowing that God used your lunch for His cause.

Fresh Water for Dry Souls

John 7:37-39

Introduction

A. There is nothing like a hot, dry summer to help us to understand the message of this text. During a hot, dry spell everything suffers. Hot and dry wind sucks the life out of every living thing. A good rain restores life and brings freshness again.

B. As physical life suffers in dry times, so do spiritual lives. Without the refreshing showers of blessings from God, humankind pays a dear price. God's blessings affect every area of our lives. When our souls are blessed, we have a positive attitude toward all things. God wants to give us what we need to be fully alive.

C. Jesus chose a very special time to make His offer of refreshing water. Read John 7:37-39.

I. The Feast of Tabernacles Was One of the Great Days for the Jews

A. The Feast of Tabernacles was celebrated for seven days each fall to help them remember the wilderness wanderings.

  1. It was second only to the Passover Feast in importance to the Jews.

  2. They remembered the miseries that were endured for 40 years (see Exod. 16 and 17).

B. Deliverance from the wilderness came when they took God's guidance at face value.

  1. They were in the desert because they had failed to trust God (Num. 13:26—14:4).

  2. They had forgotten the Exodus and God's power to bring blessings to those who trust Him.

  3. They were delivered when they listened and obeyed (Josh. 3:14-17).

C. Many people in our world today are living in desertlike situations.

    1. When we fail to trust God, He will not bless us.

    2. God invites everyone to come for a refreshing drink of His presence.

II. The Need to Respond to the Opportunity He Gives Us Must Not Be Missed

A. The people to whom Jesus gave the invitation needed something fresh in their lives.

    1. They lived under Roman rule.

    2. They lived under the burden of sin.

    3. They had very little pleasure in their lives.

B. Jesus had made the same offer to the woman at the well in John 4.

    1. That woman's life was as dead as the plants in the desert.

    2. Nothing she had tried had brought life or joy.

    3. She took a drink from the water Jesus offered to her, and life became beautifully alive.

    4. The people of her village saw the new life and wanted that for themselves.

III. The Fountain Is Still Flowing

A. Life without this living water is dull and dead. Illustration: Marilyn Monroe had everything but satisfaction. As living plants die without water, so do spiritual plants (people).

B. This condition would be sad if it was hopeless.

    1. The good news is there is help for anyone who will accept it.

    2. All that Jesus ever was, He still is (see Heb. 13:8).

    3. We can come to the fountain and have our lives renewed.

Conclusion

How is it with you today? Is your life dry as dust? Come, take a drink of the living water that still flows from God's fountain of life.

Revelations of Jesus

John 8:12-18, 25-36

Introduction

    A. These sermons are "walking" us through the Gospel of John where we are seeking to learn more about Jesus.

    B. In spite of His weariness, Jesus went to the people. Time was important, and Jesus wanted to touch as many people as possible. The encounter of verses 1-11 is not included in some manuscripts but is in harmony with the message of the Scriptures.

    C. Today's lesson focuses on three beautiful revelations of Jesus. Read John 8:12-18, 25-36.

I. Jesus Is Revealed as Light (v. 12)

    A. Here is the significance of this light.

        1. Remember that during the Feast of Tabernacles they were recalling their desert wanderings.

        2. Golden candelabras were lighted in the Temple to remind them of the pillar of fire that led them through a trackless wilderness.

        3. Now Jesus is saying, "I am to you what that light was to your forefathers."

    B. Jesus is the Light that will lead anyone into the Father's presence. We search in vain for peace with God until we find the light of Jesus.

    C. Jesus is the Light that clearly reveals how we are to live. Jesus tells us what the Father expects and what the cost of that lifestyle will be. Look at the Sermon on the Mount. Satan would keep us in darkness so that we would never know the bottom line until collection day.

    D. Jesus operates in full light. "Deny [yourself] and take up [your] cross and follow me" (Matt. 16:24).

II. Jesus Is Revealed as the Truth (John 8:32; 14:6).

A. As we learn the truth about what really matters in life, we see Jesus. The Pharisees offered substitutes that could never provide the peace and self-respect that Jesus gave. Satan endeavors to confuse us about what it takes to enjoy life.

B. Jesus reveals how God feels toward us and what it takes to please Him. Jesus shows Him to be a loving Heavenly Father. Jesus knows the design of your life and how you can function at your best. He will guide you to that if you will listen.

III. Jesus Is Revealed as Freedom (v. 36)

A. Where Jesus is accepted, there is freedom that cannot be experienced from any other source.

1. He freed lepers from contamination that bound and separated them from normal life.

2. He freed the blind from the prison of sightless eyes that kept them from enjoying the beauty of God's world.

3. He freed sinners from the slavery that deceived and frustrated their better selves.

B. Jesus still sets people free from the control of sin. He liberates us from sins that are physically destructive. No longer do we need to be imprisoned by Satan. See Rom. 6:6, 14, 22.

C. Since we are free from sin, we are free from the penalty of sin. See Rom. 6:23. We have eternal life because we are free from the punishment of sin.

Conclusion

In this chapter Jesus is revealed as light, truth, and freedom—three things that all of us desire in our lives. There is much darkness, confusion, and slavery in the world. But those who look to Jesus are free of all of these problems.

LESSONS FROM A BLIND MAN

John 9:1-25

Introduction

    A. In the last message from John 8, Jesus is revealed as light (v. 12), truth (v. 32), and freedom (v. 36).

    B. Today we are looking at a beautiful experience that should both encourage and enlighten us. Read 9:1-25. It is interesting to note that of the 33 miracles of Jesus, 4 had to do with opening blind eyes. Let's learn four lessons from this encounter.

I. Lesson One: Problems Are a Normal Part of Life (v. 3)

    A. We need to fully understand this truth. Satan delights in raising doubts in our minds about why difficult times come. Some misled people believe that if you have enough faith, there will be no problems in your life. That is not a biblical truth.

    B. The Bible is very clear about human miseries.

        1. The disciples were quick to assume that this man's problem was the result of someone's sin.

        2. It is true that the presence of sin in our world is the root cause of all suffering.

        3. It is also true that some children pay dearly for the sins of their parents. Verse 3 makes it clear that that is not the case in this situation.

    C. There are other passages of scripture that speak to the hardships that come. Matt. 5:45 states that hard times come to both good and bad people. The apostle Paul had his problems but found God's grace to be sufficient. Paul in 2 Cor. 4:7-10 clearly states that problems come to all believers.

II. Lesson Two: Obedience Is Vital in Order to Experience Deliverance

A. Here is an interesting side note to this point. God does not always work in the same way although the needs may be the same. In Mark 8 Jesus touched the blind man twice. In John 9 Jesus put mud on the man's eyes.

B. Jesus sometimes works in ways we do not understand.

C. Our responsibility is to simply obey His commands. Many never experience the thrill of seeing God work because they have never truly learned the joy of obedience. Obedience is the key to every miracle that Jesus performed.

III. Lesson Three: Skeptics Will Not Be Satisfied (v. 18)

A. Those who choose not to believe will not believe.

B. A person can choose to live in the foggy world of spiritual doubt.

C. When skeptics cannot find an answer that agrees with their preconceived ideas, they try to intimidate (note vv. 24-28).

IV. Lesson Four: When God Touches Us, We Know It (v. 25)

A. There were many questions that the man could not answer about Jesus. He did know the effect that his obedience to Jesus had on his life.

B. We may not have answers to all of the questions that will come. The things that truly matter are simple.

Conclusion

What are you absolutely sure of in your own life? Has He touched you?

The Good Shepherd

John 10:1-15

Introduction

A. This is the last of the public messages of Jesus. Jesus speaks to them in the most meaningful terminology imaginable. Shepherd and sheepfold were words embedded in Hebrew life and history. Everyone understood the meaning of these words, so there would be no question in the minds of the listeners about the message He was giving them. Read John 10:1-15.

B. Since we live in a different world, we do not fully comprehend the depth and beauty of the pictures Jesus painted with words. Sometimes we can get help and see things we would ordinarily miss. Let's try to grasp the picture Jesus painted.

I. The Good Shepherd Leads His Sheep (v. 4)

A. It is significant that He leads rather than drives His sheep. This means that He is sure that it is safe for His sheep to follow. Sheep do not need to "find" their way. They just need to follow the Shepherd. In the life outside of Christianity, people must cope for themselves in a hostile environment. Jesus simply says, "Follow Me."

B. The voice of the Good Shepherd is recognizable. Sheep know the voice of their shepherd. Illustration: Many flocks would gather at a well. When the shepherd was ready to leave, his sheep would hear his voice and come to him.

II. The Good Shepherd Is the Sheep's Access to Safety and Life (v. 7)

A. He is the one entrance by which the sheep can enter the fold and join the flock.

B. There is a dual message for us here. The Good Shepherd is protection and safety. His body literally becomes the door. Anything that comes upon His sheep must come over Him first. He is the only means of access to all that David meant when he wrote, "The LORD is my shepherd" (Ps. 23:1). He alone is our access to forgiveness for sins.

III. The Good Shepherd Gives Abundant Life (John 10:10)

A. Many people have a misconception of what Christianity is. They just see the negatives. And there are some. Note the Ten Commandments. We are designed by our Creator for clean, honest, wholesome living.

B. Those who follow the divine design live a life second to none.

IV. The Good Shepherd Knows His Sheep (v. 14)

A. Jesus is the Good Shepherd. In identifying himself in this manner, Jesus lays hold of the rich meaning of "Yahweh" as Israel's Shepherd, Ruler, Protector, and Caring Companion. Those who come to Him discover a sincere, loving, concerned, and caring Shepherd who is reaching out to improve their lives.

B. Jesus builds an intimate relationship with His sheep. Note the relationship that David writes about in Ps. 23. He still does this today. He has time for us. He looks us over. He checks for weaknesses. He gives a cup of refreshment. He knows our needs and cares for us accordingly.

Conclusion

It is no wonder that Jesus wanted to fix this picture in the minds of those who were listening. He wants to establish this picture in your minds as well. Do you know that the Lord is your Shepherd?

Lessons from the Death of a Friend

John 11:1-8, 33-44

Introduction

A. We have already learned some beautiful lessons from Jesus from the Gospel of John, but those we are beginning today will be even more significant in our spiritual development. The lessons in the last half of John's Gospel took place in the closing days of Jesus' life.

B. Today our lessons grow out of the very close friendship that existed between Jesus and His special friends, Mary, Martha, and Lazarus. These friends lived in Bethany, a town located two miles over the Mount of Olives from Jerusalem. There is strong evidence that Jesus went to their home often.

C. In these final days of Jesus' life, opposition had become more intense. His opponents were upset that Jesus had healed the man who had been born blind (chap. 9). As Jesus walked in the area of "Solomon's porch" (10:23, KJV), they became so hostile that He left to go to Jericho (vv. 22-39). While Jesus was in Jericho, He received word that Lazarus was seriously ill. Read John 11:1-8, 33-44.

I. Lesson One: Jesus Does Not Respond According to Human Clocks

A. This may well be one of the hardest lessons we will ever have to comprehend. Many times we assume that Jesus did not answer our prayers because His time schedule was different from ours.

B. Jesus deliberately waited two days before going to Bethany (see v. 6). Jesus wanted there to be no question about the miracle that was going to take place. Whatever else happened, God was to be glorified (see v. 4).

C. Our waiting in faith will not go unrewarded. Jesus may not respond when and in the manner I would desire, but

He does answer prayer. He went at the exact moment when His visit would be most meaningful for the family—not just at the invited time.

II. Lesson Two: Jesus Feels Our Deepest Emotions (v. 35)

A. The God we worship has tender feelings. The Gospel of Matthew says Jesus was feeling for the people (9:35), shows Jesus' compassion for the people (14:14), and portrays Jesus as weeping over Jerusalem (23:37).

B. Our God feels our deepest needs and reaches out to help us.

III. Lesson Three: Jesus Never Does for Us What We Can Do for Ourselves (John 11:39)

A. Jesus did not make them helpless. There were three things that needed to be done: the stone removed, life restored, and grave bindings removed. They could do two of these. So He had them do those. Jesus could have done it all, but His purpose is to help humankind rise to the level of life that the Creator had in mind.

B. This truth is illustrated over and over in the miracles of Jesus: the disciples letting down the net for the miraculous catch; the servants filling the water pots and carrying them to the master at the wedding feast; and so on.

C. The option is clear. Obey Jesus' instructions. Do what we can, and experience the joy of His help.

IV. Lesson Four: Jesus Gives Us What We Need Most—Himself

A. Jesus did not have to go to Bethany in order for Lazarus to be raised.

B. Jesus still gives himself to those who receive Him.

Conclusion

Through the death of Jesus' friend, Lazarus, we learn four valuable lessons: (1) He never comes too soon or too late. (2) He feels our deepest sorrow. (3) He does what we cannot do. (4) He gives us himself.

The Week That Changed the World

John 12:12-31

Introduction

    A. This chapter brings us to John's account of the week that changed the world. John gives almost one-half of this Gospel to telling it. Without this week, everything else is meaningless. Jesus was born to redeem humankind. This week that work is finished.

    B. This week gives us a clear understanding of why these events are so vital. Time is precious. Jesus knows that the final impressions of His followers are critical to the future of the Church. John carefully records what Jesus considers most important.

    C. Today's scripture encompasses Jesus' entry into Jerusalem and an encounter that took place in the Temple area. Read John 12:12-31. We will look at three important ideas presented in this passage.

I. A Day of Praise (vv. 12-13)

    A. This was the only time Jesus permitted a day of praise. Why now? Earlier in His ministry in 6:15 Jesus knew that they intended to try to make Him a "king by force." So He withdrew to a mountain. His time had not come. He allowed it this time so that the prophecy of Zech. 9:9 would be fulfilled. Something had to give way. Either the people would rejoice, or the stones would cry out.

    B. Who benefited from this experience? Jesus was not on an ego trip. He allowed the events of this day to take place for the benefit of the people. Those who know Jesus as Messiah want to lead the world in a celebration of happy living. We have learned that the Lord loves the praises of His people.

II. A Hunger Is Satisfied (John 12:20-26)

A. Everyone has a hunger for what Jesus represents. Not all people recognize this and seek what He came to give because they do not realize that He is what they need. There is a spiritual void in every person. This void will be filled with Jesus or something else.

B. The Greeks in this scripture had seen enough. Those who take time to truly listen and see Him will want Him. They may have started out as curiosity seekers, but they became finders of peace. They illustrate that those who pursue the best light they have will come to Jesus.

III. Consider the Great Exchange (vv. 25-26)

A. All of us have one life to live and one lifetime to invest in something. That investment will determine our eternal destiny.

B. We need to understand the options. The language Jesus uses is easy to understand. He is not talking about our will to live physically. He is talking about what we actually live for. To live as though the physical present is the ultimate opportunity results in that being the only pleasure that a person experiences. This life is not all there is. There is an eternity.

C. Jesus said, "Those who follow Me will be where I am." Where is He? He is in heaven (chap. 14). This great exchange has the highest stakes.

Conclusion

We have a wonderful opportunity. Jesus is lifted up before us this day. You have the opportunity to come to Him in faith. You can make Him the Lord of your life and live with Him forever if you choose to.

The New Commandment

John 13:34-35

Introduction

A. The new commandment specified in this chapter is one of the greatest attractions of Christianity.

B. To make sure that the disciples understood what He was talking about, Jesus demonstrated the attitude that they were to have with each other. He realizes that unless His followers love each other and demonstrate it, the Church will not survive. In Luke 22:24 the disciples argued over who was greatest. Love doesn't care about who is greatest. So Jesus focuses on that. It has been said that love is the essence of the divine nature. Since God is love, to have His nature, love must permeate our natures as well. Read John 13:34-35.

I. The New Commandment Jesus Gives Is Found in John 13:34

A. The Ten Commandments are 80 percent negative.

1. This commandment is totally positive and enables one to keep all of the laws of Moses.

2. This one commandment makes it simple to please God as well as to live the Christian life.

B. No one can rightfully claim to be God's child who does not keep all of the commandments, including this one.

1. The very nature of Christianity is that we are imitators of Christ.

2. If we do not keep His commandments, we do not love Him and are not His followers (see 14:15).

C. Love is the stamp of authenticity on Christianity.

1. It is true that some people are kind, good neighbors, and love others. The problem is that they do not love God. So they are not keeping all of the commandments.

2. Some people profess to be Christians but do not live warm, loving lives. Since God's nature is not theirs, they are not His.

3. Love for God and others is the distinguishing mark of discipleship.

4. A person can be religious without love but cannot be a Christian without love. It is like the difference between gold-plated jewelry and pure gold jewelry.

D. Love enables us to fulfill all of the other commandments. Love deliberately practices that which pleases the one loved.

II. In 13:1-5 Jesus Demonstrates How to Show Love

A. Service is the language of love. In this passage Jesus takes the role of a servant and washes the disciples' feet. Jesus shielded Judas from exposure because He loved him. He demonstrates His love for you and me by going to the Cross.

B. Love is something that you do. Ruth expressed her love for Naomi by staying with her. Jacob proved his love for Rachel by working 14 years. In Jesus' conversation with Peter in John 21, He told Peter to show Him that he loved Jesus. Love is still evidenced by actions rather than by words.

Conclusion

Read 1 Cor. 13 emphasizing the characteristics of love. If we are living this way, we can be sure we are keeping the commandments. If we love God, our lives will manifest that love. It is easy to be a Christian. We just love God and do what comes naturally.

Three Great Promises

John 14

Introduction

A. The setting is the last night of Jesus' life. Within a matter of hours Jesus will be hanging on a cross. His followers will be afraid for their lives. They will be greatly confused. Jesus knows that even the Resurrection will not resolve the emotional trauma they will experience. So He gives them hope. Jesus is preparing His disciples to face anything that comes their way.

B. This chapter is too often left for funerals. It does comfort us to understand the reality of heaven in times of loss. However, we do ourselves a disservice by reserving it just for times of grief. Jesus knew the anguish of a troubled spirit. So He makes a strong statement. "Have faith in God; have faith in Me" (see v. 1). If we cannot have faith in God and in Jesus, what can we believe in? If we do have faith in God and in Jesus, why are we so anxious about life? In this chapter there are three great promises. Read John 14:1-18.

I. I Will Come for You (v. 3)

A. Jesus had stated the reality of heaven (v. 2). There are many verses that describe heaven to us: "It is God's throne" and dwelling place (Matt. 5:34; 6:1). In Rev. 21:1-4 and 22:1-5, John paints beautiful word pictures. Heaven is the absence of all the things that have plagued us since the fall of humankind. Those who qualify will have a great eternal reward.

B. The promise is powerful and encouraging. "I want you to be with Me. I will come for you." Jesus says, "I will meet you at the junction of your faith and My promise to take you home with Me."

II. I Will Answer Your Prayer (John 14:13-14)

A. There is more to Christianity than the promise of heaven. Jesus is speaking to men who have great faith in Him. They have made great sacrifices to follow Him, and He wants them to know that help is available. Jesus wants us to know that today help continues to be available to us. Heaven begins when we reach the place of absolute trust in God.

B. How does this relate to the promise? The promise is not a blank check for spoiled children. The key to the promise's fulfillment is found in verse 13 where Jesus explains that this is true so that the Son may bring glory to the Father. We ask for those things we truly believe that we need subject to His wisdom, His love, and His glory. Who wants anything that an all-wise, all-loving Father does not desire for us?

III. God's Presence Within (vv. 16-18)

A. Jesus is preparing His disciples in a manner that will greatly strengthen their lives.

1. In verse 17, Jesus says, "I will be in you."
2. Then in verse 18, we read that He does not want us to struggle by ourselves.
3. While Jesus was with them, they had help for every situation.
4. Jesus knew He would be taken physically from them. Where would they get their help after He was gone?
5. Jesus wanted to let them know He would dwell within them. No one could ever take that presence away.

B. Jesus' presence within us enables us to face life with confidence and joy.

Conclusion

Note Paul's statements in 2 Cor. 4:7-9 and Rom. 8:35-39. How do we live that way? We claim these three great promises for ourselves.

THE BEAUTY OF ABIDING IN HIM

John 15:1-16

Introduction

A. This passage contains the words that Jesus spoke on the last night of His life. Chapters 13—17 indicate that it was a night of giving hope. In the middle of those evening hours we find a lesson on abiding in Him. The lesson we will study today will increase our pleasure in life once the truth grips our minds and hearts. Read John 15:1-16.

B. The truth for today is found in verse 4a. *The Living Bible* paraphrase is beautiful. "Take care to live in me, and let me live in you." That which is vitally connected to a great source of supply is privy to all of the resources of that supply. People who are living in the Vine will have the Vine living in them. That's the formula for success as a Christian.

I. What Does It Mean to Abide in Christ?

A. There are a number of things it could be: (1) To be loyal to Jesus' teaching—it is this and more. (2) To have His teachings fleshed out in our lives—it is this and more. (3) To make Him the focus of our attention, the center of our affections—it is this and more. (4) To make Him our all-absorbing concern and our all-controlling love—it is this and more.

B. To abide in Christ is to be fully ourselves. It is to live out our distinctive human lives while the fullness of Jesus flows through us. It makes me be the best "me" I can be to the glory of the Gardener. Branches attached to the same tree differ, but each brings glory to the Gardener. Illustrate with a story of how a gardener feels when he or she goes to a tree or vine and picks the fruit of his or her labors. I don't have to be like anyone else. I will be the best "me" that Jesus can enable me to be.

37

II. How Can I Carry Out the Principle of Abiding in Christ?

A. Again, there are a number of possibilities. I must read my Bible. But there is more. Prayer is an indispensable part of my life. But there is still more. Worship and interaction with other Christians is vital. But we need more.

B. God wants us to be like Jesus.

1. He was not a recluse. Jesus was where the people were—markets, shops, fields, and so on.

2. Jesus was not in hiding with the fear that His purity would be contaminated. Illustrate with the story of Jesus' visit to Matthew's house that stirred up the religious leaders of His day.

3. Jesus was constantly demonstrating the love of the Father for a hungry world.

4. We are to live the "Jesus life" in our daily routines.

C. How do we live the "Jesus life" in our daily routines? We abide in Christ by developing a keen awareness of His presence. We let His nature flow through us in any way He chooses.

D. As we live this life, those around us will be drawn to Jesus. They see us enjoying the presence of God. They see us thriving in spite of the problems of life that come to all of us. As Jesus flows through us, we will bear fruit for His honor and His glory.

Conclusion

In verse 16 Jesus said, "You did not choose me, but I chose you and appointed you to go and bear fruit—fruit that will last." Being chosen to bear fruit for His honor is one of the greatest compliments we can ever experience. It is beautiful to abide in Him.

Jesus' Plan for You

John 16:1-15

Introduction

A. In chapters 13—15 Jesus is preparing His disciples for what is coming. Chapter 13 assures them of love and understanding in this life. Chapter 14 assures them of an eternity with Him. Chapter 15 assures them that they can live meaningful lives while waiting for eternity. The scripture for today assures believers of triumphant living in the midst of trouble. Read John 16:1-15.

B. The Bible is a very frank, honest book. It tells about the foibles of its heroes. It tells of David's failure with Bathsheba in 2 Sam. 11. It tells of the disagreement between Paul and Barnabas in Acts 15. In this 16th chapter of John Jesus tells us that we will have major problems. While we do experience major problems, Jesus assures us that He will get us through these times triumphantly. On the other hand, Satan conceals the consequences of living in sin. Illustration: Tell about the prodigal son's experience in the hog pen.

C. Jesus wants His followers to know what is coming and how they will handle that future.

I. The Reason for Advance Notice Is Found in John 16:1

A. The *Amplified Bible* reads, "I have told you all these things so that you should not be offended—taken unawares and falter, or be caused to stumble and fall away, and to keep you from being scandalized and repelled." It is possible for believers to be surprised by the maneuverings of Satan and subsequently be defeated by them. God does not want us stumbling through life as a person trips over a hidden rock. His will is that we would walk tall and confidently. God wants us to produce the fruit of peace in the face of adversity.

B. Jesus knew that the pressure would be discouraging and the disciples would be tempted to give up. Verse 4 in every translation shows how Jesus alerted the disciples to the problems ahead. They did not need the warning while Jesus was with them. Since Jesus was to leave them soon, He prepared them to survive the tough times ahead.

II. How Do We Make It Through the Tough Experiences of Life? (v. 7)

A. The coming of the Comforter to indwell us will be our strength.

1. Illustration: The presence of the Spirit within us is like the existence of air in a football. You cannot put enough pressure on it to deflate it. In order to let the air out you must first puncture it.

2. The Knox translation reads, "He who is to befriend you." This means that anything that overcomes us must first encounter our indwelling Friend, the Holy Spirit. Since nothing can overcome the Holy Spirit, we can be assured of ultimate victory regardless of our circumstances.

B. Jesus stands in the presence of the Father interceding for help for us in every area of our lives.

1. Jesus will guide us in the decisions we need to make. He will make us sensitive to weaknesses that may arise in our lives (vv. 8-11).

2. The Holy Spirit will expose sin for what it is, and the more we know the true nature of the temptation, the less attractive it becomes. The reason we can live a victorious life is because of the presence of the Holy Spirit within us. Satan deceived Eve, but the Holy Spirit helps us in this battle.

Conclusion

Jesus' plan for His followers is that we live confident, victorious lives. Jesus went to the Cross to make this possible. The Holy Spirit helps us to keep the faith, and the faith keeps us.

JESUS' PRAYER FOR YOU

John 17

Introduction

A. Of all of the people who have ever lived, who would you most prefer to have pray for you? Moses had a powerful relationship with God. Elijah's power is demonstrated in mighty ways in 1 Kings 17 and 18. Paul would be an awesome choice. How about Jesus himself?

B. In John 17 Jesus is praying for all of us. In verse 20 Jesus deliberately includes us in His prayer. What Jesus prayed that night is as much for us as it was for the Twelve. Let us step into that moment as we read Jesus' prayer. Read John 17.

I. Request No. 1: "Keep Them" (See NASB)

A. Keep them in unity (v. 11).

1. Let there be a sense of "oneness" in them. Note also that in verses 21 and 23 Jesus prays again for their unity.

2. It is important to remember that Jesus is not praying for uniformity. There is a vast difference between unity and uniformity. Illustration: Discuss the unity of the different materials in an automobile that yield their individual qualities for the benefit of the whole.

3. Before the fulfillment of this prayer, there was jealousy among the disciples. After this prayer they were in one accord. (See Acts 4:32).

B. Keep them from evil (John 17:15). *The Living Bible* reads, "Keep them safe from Satan's power." Throughout Jesus' ministry He delivered people from Satan's power. Examples: Look at the woman at the well (see chap. 4) and the Gadarene demoniacs (see Matt. 8). Jesus does not want us to be pushed around by Satan. If the Father hears the Son's prayer, it is possible to win the battle with sin and Satan and live victoriously.

II. Request No. 2: "Let Them Have Joy"

A. John 17:13 in the *Amplified* reads, "I am coming to You. I say these things while I am still in the world, so that My joy may be made full and complete and perfect in them —that they may experience *My delight* fulfilled in them, that My enjoyment may be perfected in their own souls, that they may have *My gladness* within them filling their hearts" (emphasis added). Jesus delighted in fulfilling the Father's will. We should have delight and gladness in our relationship with our Father.

B. Many people have a misconception of Christianity. They see it as a negative, joy-robbing experience. It is a positive, exciting experience that should radiate on our faces.

C. For too long the lie about Christianity has prevailed. The truth is, living for Jesus offers the highest pleasure in life.

III. Request No. 3: "That They May Be Sanctified"

A. One of the key meanings of the word "sanctified" (v. 17) is "set apart for sacred use." In the same way that God used Mount Sinai for His purpose to declare himself, He also wants to use us now. Jesus was set apart to bring glory to the Father.

B. Jesus prays for us to be set apart to bring glory to the Father in our world.

Conclusion

A. Before we look at the final request, note the explanation in verse 21. Jesus wants them kept from the prison of sin so that the world might know that God is in control. He wants them kept in unity and love to show the world that Christians are different. He wants the believers to have joy and gladness to show the world that we have what it is looking for. He wants them sanctified so that His beauty can come through the crust of our humanity.

B. Jesus' fourth and final request is in verse 24. We know where He is—heaven. We want to spend eternity with Him.

C. Jesus spent some of the final moments of His life interceding with the Father with these requests. I want them to be a part of my life. How about you?

The Garden

John 18:1-11

Introduction

   A. The Garden of Gethsemane is at the foot of the Mount of Olives near the Kidron Brook. It is not far from the Sheep Gate that is so familiar in scripture passages. The garden is still there to provide a physical reminder of this scene. We are told that some of the trees can be dated back to the time of Christ.

   B. Why is this special place so well preserved despite 2000 years of wars and hostility? The garden provides four valuable truths that apply to our lives today. Read John 18:1-11.

I. Truth No. 1: There Is a Time and Place When Everyone Faces the Issue of Betrayal

   A. We will take a look at Judas, the betrayer (v. 2). Judas was no monster. But he took the decision of his relationship with Jesus too lightly. There was more at stake here. When the results were out of control, Judas was frantic (Matt. 27:3-5). Judas had associated himself with the wrong crowd. Tragedy was the result.

   B. This can happen to any of us. The process is the same when we underestimate what is at stake. The results are the same—great tragedy and heartache. There will be a time and place for each of us to evaluate our relationship with Christ.

II. Truth No. 2: In the Garden Jesus Demonstrated How Much He Cared

   A. Jesus intervened for the freedom of all who believe in Him (John 18:4-9). Jesus deliberately chose to pay the price of redemption (Luke 22:42-44). He chose to physically lay His life on the line.

B. Another demonstration of His caring concern is found in John 18:10-11. In Luke 22:51 we read that Jesus healed the man's ear. There is no clearer example of caring love than this. In the garden Jesus reveals how much He loves each one of us.

III. Truth No. 3: The Garden Was a Place of Renewal for the Disciples

A. According to John 18:2, Jesus often went to the garden with His disciples. They learned a lot from Jesus as He taught in the Temple, synagogues, and marketplaces. The greater lessons may have been learned in the privacy of the garden and the seclusion of the desert.

B. We need a quiet place where Jesus can reveal things to us that we cannot hear in a crowd. This private spot will become our place of renewal. Either you will find a place of refreshment, or you will burn out. Illustration: Even the strongest of metals must be taken off the grinding stone at some point, or it will lose its strength.

IV. Truth No. 4: Jesus Knew That Some Would Respond to the Invitation and Others Would Coldly Walk Away

A. This is more clearly described in Luke 22:40-44.

B. For the sake of those who would respond, Jesus surrendered everything.

Conclusion

Each one of us needs a trip to the "garden of surrender." We must be sure that our garden experience is not one of betrayal. When we care enough to respond to what Jesus did for us, something special happens. The garden of our hearts becomes a place of sweet communion with Him.

Behold Calvary!

John 19:1-18

Introduction

    A. The purpose of the chapters prior to this one has been to help us gain a greater appreciation for the events of the last hours of the life of Christ. The scripture we are looking at today brings us face-to-face with the heart of the entire matter—the death of Jesus. Read John 19:1-18.

    B. "Behold the man!" (KJV). In verse 5 Pilate unknowingly and unintentionally underscored one of the greatest needs of humankind—to give attention to Jesus. Behold means to become aware of, to gain an understanding, to watch carefully with attention to details of behavior for the purpose of arriving at a judgment. Pilate is simply saying, "Get all of the facts. Make an intelligent decision." Today I ask you to carefully consider the truth and make an intelligent judgment.

I. Behold the Man of Calvary! (v. 5)

    A. Who is He? (1) Mary's Son, the Carpenter from Nazareth. (2) The Miracle Worker whose deeds could not be explained away. (3) The Teacher who revealed simple revelations of God to them. (4) A Friend to all of the people.

    B. But Jesus is more than this. Look at the great confession by Peter in Matt. 16:13-16. Jesus is the Son of God, Mediator between earth's humanity and heaven's holiness. He is the Lamb slain from the foundation of the world—the sacrifice for our sins. He is the Great High Priest moved with the feelings of our infirmities. Pilate did not know to whom he was calling their attention, but we do.

II. Behold the Exchange That Took Place! (John 18:38-40)

    A. Pilate assumed they would make an intelligent choice. He knew that Jesus was innocent (v. 38). Pilate knew that

Barabbas was guilty of many sins. Pilate assumed that the people would make an intelligent choice. The people chose guilt over innocence.

B. How could they have made such a choice? They did not carefully consider all of the facts. We are making the same choice. Be sure to get the facts.

III. Behold the Three Crosses! (John 19:17-18)

A. The center Cross upon which Jesus hung represents the truth—God loves you and me. Remember, we are all included personally in the events and teachings of the final hours of Jesus' life. While God loves the whole world, He loves you and me individually. The enemies of Christ look at the Cross and see the fruit of their actions. What do you see when you look at the Cross?

B. One of the side crosses is the symbol of the rejection of divine mercy. What do you think when you look and listen to this man and his response? Do you wonder why he was not penitent like the other thief?

C. The third cross demonstrates penitence and pardon. Look and you will see how simple it is to know forgiveness (Luke 23:42-43). This cross demonstrates for all humankind for all time how much God desires to forgive us.

D. Behold the crosses. You and I are either on one or the other of the side crosses.

Conclusion

A. Behold the results of this entire scene. "It is finished!" (John 19:30). The plan of redemption has been completed. No one ever has to be lost again.

B. We are free to revel in the fellowship of a God who created us for himself and would not give up until each one of us has that privilege.

C. Pilate said, "Behold—take a good look. Make an intelligent decision." So I challenge you this day, "Take a good look—make your eternal decision!"

No Cause for Sorrow

John 20:1-18

Introduction

A. Jesus Christ died the most terrible death imaginable. It is impossible to think of a more cruel, inhumane death than this. His followers were heartbroken, and a dark cloud of sorrow hung over their lives. Then came Sunday—and the resurrection of Jesus! In one miraculous moment, God the Father raised His Son. By this He broke the grip of sorrow on the lives of those who follow Him.

B. Was Jesus really dead? Some have attempted to explain away the miracle of the Resurrection by claiming that He was not dead. Without a death there can be no resurrection. Consider these facts. These men were well trained in the act of execution (19:32-34). The Roman centurion was a professional soldier, and Pilate believed his report (Mark 15:42-45). Those who had the most to lose by a resurrection were satisfied that Jesus was dead (Matt. 27:62-66).

C. When Sunday came, it was the greatest day in the history of the world. Read John 20:1-18. In one miraculous moment gloom, despair, and defeat are blown away.

D. This experience is as well documented as any other event in human history.

I. The Evidence of the Resurrection

A. The tomb was empty (vv. 1-2). They had seen Him buried. Now He was gone. Because of the Roman guards, His body could never have been stolen as accused. If His disciples had stolen His body, what about the grave clothes? (vv. 6-7).

B. There was the report of the guards (Matt. 28:11-15). If there was a logical explanation, why not simply state the facts? The enemies of Jesus had been satisfied with the security of the tomb (27:66).

C. There were 10 recorded appearances of the resurrected Jesus: (1) to Mary Magdalene (John 20); (2) to the 3 women (Luke 24); (3) to the 2 travelers on the road to Emmaus (Luke 24); (4) to Peter as reported by Paul (1 Cor. 15); (5) to the 10 behind closed doors (John 20); (6) To the 11—including Thomas (John 20); (7) to the 7 beside the sea when they had fished all night (John 20); (8) to the group of 500 as Paul records (1 Cor. 15); (9) to James (1 Cor. 15); (10) to the 11 just before the Ascension.

D. The greatest evidence for us involves more recent experiences with the resurrected Christ.

  1. Changed lives of people since that time

    a. John Newton—a drunken sailor who became the writer of "Amazing Grace"

    b. Chuck Colson—a lying, manipulative politician who became the director of a prison ministry

  2. The very survival of the Church in the face of an all out effort to destroy it.

II. The Meaning of the Resurrection to Us Today

A. We realize that being in a right relationship with God does not deliver us from all problems. This relationship does assure us of ultimate victory. While the devil seems to win at times, God has a plan for the final victory. Ultimately we win!

B. The Resurrection means that there is hope for hopeless moments. Illustration: Look what happened with the two men on the road to Emmaus. He will do the same for each one of us. In our darkest hours, we can hold on. Sunday is just a light ray away.

III. The Resurrection Validates All We Believe

A. The angel said, "Give him the name Jesus" (Matt. 1:21). These are just words without the Resurrection. The Resurrection is the stamp of authenticity on God's forgiveness for our sins.

B. Jesus cried, "It is finished" (John 19:30). This means salvation has been made available to all of us. The Resurrection validates this. The Resurrection means that God is more powerful than Satan.

Conclusion

A. "Come and see the place where [the Lord] lay" (Matt. 28:6).

B. Go! Share the good news. He is risen!

JESUS STILL CARES

John 21:1-17

Introduction

A. The redemption of humankind has been completed. Those who want forgiveness for their sins can experience the beauty of a Christian life. God has used the cross of Jesus to bridge the chasm that had separated Him from humankind. To verify His power over Satan, the Resurrection has taken place.

B. What happens now? Will God allow human beings to struggle through life on their own strength? No. He will still be present to help those who choose to have faith in Him. Read John 21:1-17.

C. I remind you that Jesus is eternally the same (Heb. 13:8). Paul discovered this truth while on a ship in a serious storm (Acts 27:23-25). Millions have found that in their midnight hours Jesus is nearby. Illustrate with a story of how the Lord helped someone through a difficult situation.

I. Jesus Cares About Our Frustrations (John 21:3-5)

A. Peter and those with him discovered this great truth. Because of the confusion of the past days, Peter wanted to do something familiar that he could enjoy. When he caught nothing, his frustration increased. Jesus knew what was happening with His followers and cared. The Master revealed himself and met their needs.

B. Jesus cares about the frustrations we experience today.
   1. There are some days when nothing seems to go right. He tells us we don't have to be successful. We just need to love Him.
   2. The frustrations that come from strained relationships can be resolved.
   3. We will experience frustrations in this world. But He

said, "Be of good cheer. I have overcome the world" (16:33, KJV).

II. Jesus Cares About Our Physical Needs (21:9-13)

A. Peter and His friends needed more than words. They needed physical help for their tired, weary bodies. Jesus is more practical than some would acknowledge. He didn't ask if they wanted food. He had it ready and waiting for them.

B. Jesus still cares about our physical needs today. Sometimes the most spiritual thing we can do is to take care of our bodies. Sometimes He touches us physically. Other times He wants us to help ourselves.

III. Jesus Cares About the Quality of Our Lives (vv. 15-17)

A. There is much more to a good life than physical conditions or emotional feelings. To be the best it can be, life must have purpose and meaning.

   1. Jesus gave Peter an assignment to complete. He is saying to Peter, "I need your help."
   2. Jesus knew that Peter needed to be needed.
   3. Jesus is simply saying, "Demonstrate your love in the life that you live."

B. When we feel needed and successful in fulfilling that need, the quality of our lives is dramatically improved.

   1. Most of us will never be superstars in the spiritual world. We can fulfill the challenge Jesus gave to Peter.
   2. Love God, live like it, and in doing that experience fulfillment. Your assignment is simple. Your reward is great.

Conclusion

Jesus cares about you and everything that happens in your life. He did not leave us alone to struggle for victory in our own strength. He is very real in this present world. The hymn "Does Jesus Care" says, "O yes, He cares; I know He cares!"

He Is Life

John 6:22-48

Introduction

A. The setting of this scripture lesson is important. It follows the great miracle of the feeding of 5,000 and Jesus' refusal to let them make Him king. After that miracle Jesus appeared to the disciples on a stormy sea, and we learn two lessons. He knows where you are even if you don't. According to Mark 6:51, Jesus brings peace for stormy situations.

B. Jesus is especially interested in those who seek Him for himself rather than for selfish reasons. Look at John 6:26. We need to learn this very important lesson. Those who seek Him will have Him.

C. Jesus uses the encounter to teach a lesson that lies at the very heart of the Bible. Eternal life is available for all who come to Him. Eternal life has already begun. Once born, we never cease to exist somewhere. Read John 6:22-48.

I. Let's Take a Look at Life As It Is Today

A. With some people, life is chaotic. They seem to go from one problem to another. About the time they think they're getting the puzzle of life together, someone bumps the table. Life is not kind to them. The harder they work, the more there is to do.

B. With some people, life is momentarily good. All of the things they believe to be necessary are in place—health, job, friends, and so on. Illustrate: Some people appear to be very happy when they respond to music, but then the music stops.

C. Life now, whatever it is, is temporary. What then should our attitude be? We need to hold everything of this world loosely whether good or not so good. This is the lesson of verse 27. We should pursue the good life in Christ that never ceases.

II. Jesus Provides Eternal Life Now (vv. 39-40)

A. This is the purpose for which Jesus came into the world. The life of the harvest does not wait until the plant dies. It is determined while the plant is still alive. People were created for God. Those who develop as He intended fulfill His purpose, and He blesses them. Jesus came to give abundant life now (3:17 and 10:10).

B. Eternal life begins now. Once we die, no more decision can be made. Jesus makes life beautiful now, and that makes eternity's prospects exciting.

III. How Do We Gain or Come into This Life?

A. It is found in response to the drawing power of Jesus. According to 6:44, 65, we are drawn into the Kingdom but never dragged into it. Those who go to heaven are attracted by the courting power of Jesus and come to Him of their own choosing.

B. Jesus alone is our means of gaining life. There are many means of satisfying one's religious hunger. Religions abound throughout the world. Jesus has the key to eternal life (v. 68 and Acts 4:12).

Conclusion

A. There is a heaven to be gained. Jesus talked about a place He has prepared for us (John 14). In Revelation, John tries to describe it for us as best he can.

B. Wise is the person who recognizes how temporary life on this earth is and yields to the Holy Spirit who draws him or her to eternal life in God's presence.

C. Illustration: A caterpillar wraps itself in a cocoon that will be shed later so that it can enter into a more beautiful life than it could ever have experienced crawling around a tree. We yield to the protective custody of Jesus and enter a glorious life through Him.

A Matter of Seeing

John 9:1-11

Introduction

A. Seeing is a natural function of the human life that sometimes needs attention. Some people are born blind. As we grow older in life, our vision dims and we have to have help to see. Sometimes we will get foreign matter in our eyes and need help to get it out.

B. Our spiritual sight functions in much the same way. Sometimes there is a gradual deterioration that takes place in our spiritual sight. Sometimes foreign matter gets into our spiritual eyes and obstructs our vision. Some people, like the man in this passage, have never been able to see. There is help available in every situation. Read John 9:1-11. There are three vital lessons to be learned from this scripture.

I. Lesson One: Blindness Is Not Always a Matter of Sin (vv. 2-3)

A. The disciples followed the old philosophy that the man's blindness was God's punishment for someone's sins. Remember the complaint of Job's comforter in Job 4:7. In John 9:3 Jesus is saying that it is not always that simple.

B. Our spiritual sight is not always a simple matter. There are some gray areas in human behavior where we must rely on the guidance of the Holy Spirit.

1. The Ten Commandments are basic and nondebatable.
2. The church body gives us some guidelines to help us in tricky areas.
3. In other areas there is room for special conviction, with the question being, not what can I do and get by with, but how best can I glorify Jesus?

C. How do we handle these decisions? This is done by staying close and sensitive to God.

II. Lesson Two: Jesus Wants Us to See (vv. 6-7)

A. Jesus wants us to walk without fear. Four of His miracles related to blind persons: (1) the blind man of the present passage; (2) two blind men (Matt. 9:27); (3) a blind man at Bethsaida (Mark 8:22); and (4) the blind man near Jericho (Mark 10:46).

1. To walk in twilight is dangerous. To walk in darkness guarantees disaster.

2. Walk with Jesus and walk in light (John 8:12).

B. Spiritual blindness is dangerous. Jesus wants us to think, analyze, compare, and see the truth. Satan loves darkness and twilight so that he can keep people confused. Common sense understands the wisdom of walking in the light of Jesus.

III. Lesson Three: Obedience Brings Sight (9:11)

A. Obedience is a prerequisite to seeing. In this passage Jesus told the man to wash his eyes (v. 7). He obeyed, and he was able to see. He told Bartimeus to get up and go (Mark 10:52). In Acts 9 Paul's sight was restored when he obeyed God's instructions.

B. The better we obey, the more we can see. Most of us do not need more light. We just need to walk in the light we already have.

Conclusion

We must frankly face spiritual blindness.

1. Some people have never seen. For them, there is a whole new world waiting to be discovered.

2. Some people are afflicted with the sudden distractions that come into their lives and are unable to handle the difficulties.

3. Many people have the problem of gradual deterioration because they fail to stay sensitive to God's guidance.

4. How is the eyesight of your heart?

Lessons from an Unusual Experience

John 12:1-11

Introduction

A. This is the week prior to the death of Jesus. Passover is only days away, and this will be a Passover unlike any ever experienced. This has been described as the week that changed the world.

B. The events of our scripture passage took place in Bethany at the home of Simon the Leper (see Matt. 26:6). The resurrection of Lazarus has recently taken place, and he is present (John 12:2). This supper could have been prepared to celebrate the raising of Lazarus, or it may have been just a normal gathering of friends. It took place in the evening following the Sabbath.

C. The events of that evening offer three very important lessons. Read John 12:1-11.

I. Lesson One: Love Is an Extravagant Reality

A. Let us consider the nature of love. Love is not a feeling or experience or a condition. Love is something you do regardless of how you feel or what the conditions may be.

B. Love is extravagant in its action.

1. What Mary did in verse 3 was the equivalent of spending a year's income. The action of verse 3 was spontaneous.

2. Love does not have to be coaxed. It is anxious to display itself.

3. A year's wages poured out unsolicited said, "I love you." When was the last time you did something for God just to say, "I love you"?

C. Love produces an abandonment of self-consciousness (v. 3). Mary anointed His feet with oil. The work of a servant was to meet his master when he came home from a journey so that he could wash his feet with water. Without request, Mary took the role of a servant. She was oblivious to what anyone thought. We need to come to the same place in our lives today.

II. Lesson Two: There Is an Exposure of Hypocrisy (vv. 4-6)

A. Hypocrisy always hides behind others. In this passage Judas hides behind the needs of the poor. Hypocrites always deal in the mystery of others.

B. Hypocrisy is selfish. Judas wanted the money in the bag he carried. True love would have said, "Isn't it great that she cares so much for the Master?" Real love rejoices at any opportunity to glorify Jesus.

C. Hypocrisy preys on what should be one's strength. Our greatest strength has the potential of being our greatest weakness.

III. Lesson Three: Now Is the Time to Honor Jesus with Love (vv. 7-8)

A. There are some things we can do almost anytime, while others must be grasped at the moment of opportunity. There are always times to do some things, even good things. That which is expedient must be done today.

B. It is imperative that I demonstrate my love for Jesus today. I do not know how long I have to show my love for Him. If I can do the other things, I will. But I must know that I have lived my life filled with love for Jesus. Many have intended to do this but never accomplish that goal. Life is uncertain.

Conclusion

This was an unusual experience that evening in Bethany. It was rich in meaning. We need to make this a very unusual day in our lives by determining that we will demonstrate our love for Jesus.

WHOSE TRIAL IS THIS?

John 18:15-27

Introduction

    A. Sometimes when we watch a trial scene it is difficult to determine who is being tried. Witnesses are sometimes badgered in such a way that you wonder if they are on trial. We are looking at a situation just like that.

    B. The last night before Calvary was rapidly passing. The events of the evening are gathering momentum. Jesus has eaten His final meal. He has washed the disciples feet. He has prayed for them. He has gone to the garden to talk with His Father, and from there He will be taken to trial.

    C. This trial is a mockery of every legal procedure known to law. But we are looking here at another trial that is taking place. We cannot identify with the trial of Jesus, but we can with this one. Read John 18:15-27.

I. There Are Some Things to Note in Defense of Peter

    A. Peter was the only one to defend the Master in the garden. According to Luke 22:38, there were two swords but only Peter used his. Peter was ready to die for Jesus (Matt. 26:33-35).

    B. He followed Jesus into the house of Caiaphas (see John 18:15). Only Peter and John dared to go that far. No one knew what was truly happening. Why would Peter take such a chance? He genuinely loved Jesus. He had left a good business to follow Jesus.

    C. Peter's intentions and record up to this point were good.

II. Peter Failed at What Appeared to Be the Most Critical Moment of All

    A. We look at Peter's three denials.

        1. The first one was easy as he moved through the door

(vv. 16-17). The second denial came as he stood in the company of the servants and officers (v. 25). The third came as he was still standing by the soldier's fire (note Matt. 26:74).

2. Note the progression of Satan's challenge. At first Peter handled it well. By the third denial Peter was in deep trouble.

B. The problem is clear. What began as a good thing, "following Jesus" (John 18:15), deteriorated rapidly. According to Luke 22:54, "Peter followed at a distance." Peter warmed himself at the enemy's fire.

C. There are many who follow this formula today. They love God and believe in Jesus but follow at a distance. Many are afraid of the enemy and fail to live in Rom. 12:2. Christianity is plagued by "a cult of softness."

D. We need a clear sense of identities and priorities.

1. Christianity is corrupted by a passion for pleasure and possessions.

2. In many cases we are little different from those who make little place for Jesus.

3. Someone has said, "In the midst of a world screaming for answers to life Christians are stuttering."

Conclusion

A. Peter's own heart cried, "Guilty!" According to Luke 22:62, "he went outside and wept" bitter tears of repentance. At his next trial in Acts 4, Peter passed with flying colors.

B. Jesus is not on trial in our world. We are. The issue of who He is and what He does has been settled forever. We are on trial to witness for Him. It has been said that Christianity is an epic for heroes only. I want to be a hero for Jesus. What about you?

So Send I You

John 20:19-23

Introduction

    A. Some of the disciples' best experiences with Jesus were after the Resurrection: (1) the appearance to two men on the road to Emmaus; (2) the appearance to Mary in the garden; (3) the appearance to the disciples after they had fished all night.

    B. Every revelation of Jesus carried a compulsion to service. There is a desire and responsibility to share this good news with others. When we have the presence of the resurrected Lord in our lives, then we, too, have a compulsion to serve. Read John 20:19-23.

I. A Frank Look at the Disciples

    A. They were fearful and justifiably so. They had just seen Jesus treated cruelly, and they expected the same treatment. In the midst of a frightening situation, Jesus came to them (v. 19).

    B. This wonderful experience carries the challenge of verse 21. Two great truths are present here. "As the Father has sent me, I am sending you." Great blessing carries great responsibility.

II. Truth No. 1: "As the Father Sent Me"

    A. Why was Jesus sent into the world? The Father wanted humankind to know of His love. The Father wanted humankind to have a chance to be freed from sin. The Father sent Jesus so that all humankind everywhere might be saved. Jesus sends us to carry this message to our community.

    B. How was Jesus sent?

        1. It is important to know that Jesus was not sent alone: "I and the Father are one" (10:30); "Anyone who has seen me has seen the Father" (14:9); "just as you are

in me and I am in you" (17:21). We are not sent alone into the world.

2. Jesus was dependent on the Father. He called upon the Father in the raising of Lazarus (11:41). Nothing turned Jesus aside from His assignment in the world. Therefore, we do not dare to be deterred from His assignment for us in the world.

III. Truth No. 2: "As the Father Has Sent Me, I Am Sending You"

A. This is a personal message to each one of us. While it represents everyone, it is focused on each one. The assignment will require some sacrifice on our part.

B. Christianity can never be imposed. It must be imparted. Light can only be extended. Those who follow the assignment become lights in a darkened world. Illustration: On a dark night a single light can be seen for miles.

C. The assignment is still a call to follow Jesus' example in the world. Recall the example in Gethsemane where Jesus died to His will. Consider the example on Calvary where He paid the supreme price. In order to be like Jesus we, too, must submit our wills to the call of telling others about the Father's love.

D. Jesus was sent to an uncomfortable death on a cross in order to change the world. What He came to do could not be done in comfort. We cannot do what needs to be done in our world without moving out of our comfort zones.

Conclusion

A. Some people wonder why sin is so rampant and why God doesn't do something. He cannot do anything because we will not. Augustine said, "Without us, God will not. Without God, we cannot."

B. We are sent with God's help to change our world by sharing the news of His love.

Do You Love Me?

John 21:15-22

Introduction

A. There was something very special about the experience in this scripture passage. Jesus had demonstrated His love for His followers by being present at their point of need. He met not only their emotional needs but also their physical needs.

B. In today's scripture Jesus moves into a critical area of need for people who want to make the most of their lives. He has clearly established the fact that He loves humankind. Jesus now wants them to express their love for Him. Read John 21:15-22.

I. Love Is a Two-Way Street

A. It is one thing to be loved. It is something very special to return that love. Jesus is giving Peter the opportunity to demonstrate his love. Jesus is saying, "Peter, forget the past. I want you to make the most of your life."

B. Jesus was not concerned with what had happened. He was concerned with the "now." Many people live in the past—good and bad. You can get past your past. The value of our relationship is determined by our present love for Jesus.

II. Many of Us Are the Beneficiaries of a Rich Heritage

A. Some of us have spent most of our lives in the Church. We must not live on past experiences in the Church.

B. Many of us have a rich personal heritage. We may have been blessed to live in a Christian home. We may have personally served the Lord well for years. The question for each of us to ask is, "What is happening now in my spiritual life?"

C. The question Jesus asked is, "Do you love me now?" He asked that of Peter. He asks that of us.

III. Peter Became Upset with Jesus' Persistence

A. Jesus was not punishing Peter. There may have been some significance in Jesus' asking Peter, "Do you love me?" Jesus wanted Peter to understand what really matters.

B. "Do you truly love me more than these?" (v. 15). More than the boats, the fishing nets, and so on? More than you love these, your friends? Jesus is saying, "I will have no competition for your heart.

C. I want to ask you today, "Do you truly love Jesus?"

   1. Jesus had said to Peter, "If you love Me, live like it. Let it affect your life." If we truly love Jesus, we will live like it and let that love affect our lives.

   2. Service is the language of love. A person can serve without loving, but we cannot love without serving. Illustration: When we love someone, we love doing things for him or her.

IV. Jesus Told Peter That Love Is More than a Word—He Said, "Feed My Sheep"

A. In other words, Jesus was saying, "Live as if you love Me." Peter had said, "You know all things" (v. 17). Jesus is saying, "Show me!" The life of a shepherd revolves around his sheep. Jesus is saying, "Let your life revolve around those for whom I died." He is saying, "Peter, I am giving a simple plan so that you can demonstrate your love for Me."

B. We have a simple plan through which we demonstrate our love for Jesus. We let His love affect our lives in every way. We are faithful, supportive, and committed to what we love.

Conclusion

Peter looked for a loophole (v. 21). Jesus closed it. He said, "Your responsibility is to demonstrate your love for Me." My question is, "Do you love Jesus enough to demonstrate that love in your life?"

Joshua 24:24